LANCING
A Pictorial History

A view of Lancing from the sea including the *Three Horseshoes* Inn on the left, the Grammar School buildings in the centre and the Terrace to the right. Drawing made in 1858.

LANCING

A Pictorial History

George W. Shaw

PHILLIMORE

1982

Published by
PHILLIMORE & CO. LTD.,
London and Chichester

Head Office: Shopwyke Hall,
Chichester, Sussex, England

ISBN 0 85033 455 1

This book is dedicated to the older residents of Lancing and in particular to: Mr. Tom Boyd; Mrs. Sally Duxfield; Mrs. Annie Green; Miss Gertie Hibdidge; Mrs. Eileen Long; Mrs. Kate Matten; Mr. and Mrs. Charlie White; the late Archie Colbourne and the late Steve Stringer.

Printed and bound in Great Britain by
BILLING & SONS LIMITED
Guildford, London, Oxford, Worcester

LIST OF ILLUSTRATIONS

ACKNOWLEDGEMENTS

Many people have contributed to this book by lending photographs and my thanks go to the following:

Mr. W. L. Attrell; Mrs. F. Badcock; Sister Ivy Baldock; Mr. T. G. Bashford; Mr. C. Bristow; the late Mr. Frank Broadhurst; Mr. Tom Boyd; Mr. Richard Chorley; the late Archie Colbourne; the Rev. John Cotton; Mrs. J. E. Edwards of Penhill Road; Mrs. Eve Farrant; Mr. and Mrs. Brian Finch; Mr. Cecil Gammans; Mrs. Annie Green; Mr. R. Green; Mr. Will Harman; Miss Daisey Humphrey; Mrs. D. Jenkins; Mr. and Mrs. Harry Kershaw; Lancing College Archives; Lancing Parish Council; Lancing Womens' Institute; Mrs. Eileen Long; Mr. Roland Lelliott; Miss M. Marriott; Mrs. Kate Matten; Mr. Charles Morris; Miss I. O. Neil; Mr. Brian Old; Mr. John Oxborough; Mr. Cecil Peters; Mrs. Dorothy Pipe; Mrs. Ralph Piper; Miss Mary Sear; Mr. Alfred Strudwick; the late Steve Stringer; Mr. Jack Thornberry; Mr. A. Weaver; Mr. and Mrs. Charlie White and Mr. Wilmshurst of Boundstone Close.

I would also like to thank the Director of the Public Record Office for permission to publish the document relating to Grants Manor, plate 45, and to the Editor of *Worthing Herald* for plates 103, 246, 247.

My special thanks for their generous help and encouragement go to my colleague Mr. Basil Handford; to Dr. Timothy Hudson, Editor in Sussex of the *Victoria County History*; to Mr. Ron Kerridge and to Mrs. Patricia Gill the County Archivist and her staff at the Record Office. My wife and family have, as always on these occasions, been very patient with me!

PREFACE

The village of Lancing is actually two communities—North Lancing and South Lancing. The original centre was North Lancing with its Norman church, manor and cluster of old houses. Its inhabitants were traditionally known as 'Rooks'.

There was no such nucleus in South Lancing, but a single road called Streetend led to the beach. The inhabitants of its few scattered dwellings were known as 'Seagulls'. This road joined the one running through North Lancing to Sompting, Worthing and Arundel in the west and to Shoreham via the old wooden bridge in the east. It is only during the present century that the prolific building of houses has produced a solid block of dwellings stretching from the beach without a break to the top of the downs, so taking away the peaceful village atmosphere which must have pervaded the area over the centuries.

The last 50 years have seen the transition of a rural community where horticulture was the main occupation, to a large town with engineering and other industries. The market gardens have gone, to be replaced by avenues of rather undistinguished dwellings and a major arterial road now slices north from south. One hundred years ago the population was about 800, but it stands at nearly 17,000 today.

Lancing is fortunate in having been the home of the McCarthy family, several members of which were photographers; between them they made an extensive record of the village in the early years of the century. Many of the present pictures were taken by the McCarthy brothers.

The present book is in some ways an extension of Ron Kerridge's excellent *History of Lancing* published in 1979 and includes new material which has come to light since that time. However, its main function is to preserve some of the photographic records of Lancing before they are lost for ever; hence the period covered is mainly from the present century.

There will undoubtedly be mistakes of identity, time or place and I will be very pleased to hear from anyone who can correct such faults.

Grants Manor   GEORGE W. SHAW
Lancing   1982

1. The Old Vicarage and garden, ca. 1880 with the Revd. Frederick Fisher Watson and two ladies, one of whom was probably his daughter, Margaret (1865 - 1958). His wife Margaret (Gibson) died aged 24, three weeks after their daughter was born.

ROOKS
North Lancing

2. A drawing of the church entitled 'Lancing near Brighton' by the Brighton artist Montague Penley (*see also* Nos. 68 and 90). Much artistic licence has been exercised here. Whilst a lot of the detail is quite accurate, some major features are equally inaccurate, eg. the belfry stairs are on the north side of the tower, the stone tracery in the west window is wrong and the isles windows have been omitted. Penley's initials appear on the gravestone the third from the left.

I THE PARISH CHURCH OF ST. JAMES-THE-LESS

Domesday Book contains no mention of a church in Lancing, but from the architectural evidence it has been concluded that the original church was built about 1120, and the Transitional porch was added in about 1180. A great deal of rebuilding took place between 1280 and 1300, but since that time little has changed except for the addition of a pyramidal cap to the tower in 1618 after the removal of the parapet. The church is an excellent example of the Transitional style from Early English to Decorated, and the very slight modern modifications do not detract from its early simplicity.

Two early drawings of the church by unknown artists. Both, within their limits are accurate representations.

3. (*above*) This drawing is dated 1801 and shows the west end of the church, and also the cottages, now gone, to the west.

4. (*right*) This view from the south east gives further confirmation of the presence of the cottages to the west of the church.

5. The church and Manor Road in 1910. To the left is Friar's Acre, at that time known as Newman's Farmhouse, and to the right Church Farm Cottages, now gone.

6. Three of the four bells in Lancing Church belfry were cast in the 17th century. The first one is inscribed *Gloria Deo in excelsis B. E. 1633* and two others have inscribed upon them *Bryan and William Eldridge made mee 1660.* The photograph was taken in 1935 when a fourth bell, a tenor, the gift of Mrs. K. M. Mason was added.

7. The origin of this picture is obscure, but it is inscribed: 'Interior of a cottage at Lancing near the church'. It appears to have a very large bread oven, and was probably a bakery. The cottage, no longer in existence, could have been the one to the west of the church and is seen in plates 3 and 4.

8. (*right*) The church interior in 1880. At that time the wooden reredos was still present behind the alter, and the rood screen had not yet been installed.

Lancing vicars 1834 - 1933

9. The vicar of Lancing, the Revd. Thomas Nash M.A. (Cantab) died in 1834 aged 36. He was succeeded by the Revd. Fisher Watson (*below left*) who was vicar from 1834 to 1860. He was buried on 28 August 1873 aged 83. His wife Louisa Sarah was buried on 16 December 1865 aged 72. They seem to have had two children, Harriet who died in 1838 aged 19, and Frederick Fisher who followed his father as vicar.

10. (*below right*) Frederick Fisher Watson M.A. (Cantab) was vicar from 1860 until his death on February 8 1883 at the age of 51 years. He had one daughter, Margaret, who was born on 7 March 1865. Unfortunately his wife Margaret (Gibson) died in 1865.

12. The Revd. Edward Curphey Paton succeeded Mr. Peel in 1920 and retired in September 1933. During his ministry, the church in South Lancing, St. Michaels, was built, with the Revd. R. A. Hodges as vicar. Mr. Paton died in 1958. Mrs. Paton died in 1978 in her 102nd year.

11. The Revd. Edmund Peel M.A. (Cantab) was vicar for 37 years. He is still remembered with affection by the older residents of Lancing. His wife Hannah Gertrude died on 20 April 1920 aged 68 years, and he died on 10 January 1929 aged 77 years.

13. *(above)* The church choir in 1908. Back row *(left to right)*: Owen Tee, George Searle, Will Dann, Steve Stringer, Alfred Strudwick, Mr. Walter G. Heaton, headmaster of the school, choirmaster and organist; middle row: (?), Henry Steer, John Dann, Fred Scott, Frank Aldridge; front row: Cyril Heaton, Ernest Payne, Eddie Feldwick, Leonard Heaton.

14. *(Opposite below)* This photograph of the church choir was taken in 1887 soon after Charles Stringer had taken over as parish clerk from his father Stephen. Stephen Stringer became parish clerk in 1856, a post which he held until his death at the age of 79 years, in 1887. His son, Charles (born 1840) then held the appointment until his death when his own son, Stephen (born 1899) became parish clerk until his own death at the age of 80 years in 1979. Thus the family were parish clerks for a total of 123 years. Back row *(left to right)*: Mr. Cook, James Broomfield, (?), Tom Butler, Will Saunders, Revd. Edmund Peel, (?), George Cass, (?), Edward Marshall, William Marriott (Choirmaster), Charles Stringer; middle row: (?), (?), (?), (?); front row: Butler twins, (?), (?), (?).

II LANCING MANOR

Lancing Manor House grew by alterations and additions from a small house, formerly known as the Whitehouse, or Gents, in the late 16th or early 17th century to a substantial mansion at the time of its destruction in 1972.

The first reference so far located is 'a sale in 1652 by Edward Hyde of Launcing, Yeoman, to Richard Streater of Broadwater for £300 of a messuage called Whitehouse otherwise Gents, with barns etc and 38 acres in North and South Launcing. Also a messuage and smith's forge with garden called Christmas in North Launcing in the occupation of Thomas Woods'. The alternative name of Gents suggests that the house was originally built by the Gent family, which is represented in the parish registers from 1568 to 1733.

In 1669 Richard Streater's son John mortgaged Whitehouse or Gents and 38 acres, Christmas and Burrows to John Cooke of Goring for £150, and six years later began the association between the Lloyd family and this estate in Lancing. At that time (1705) the Revd. James Lloyd of Clapham leased for one year from John Cooke the Whitehouse, 62 acres and the smithy. Some time between 1705 and 1711 the Revd. Lloyd must have purchased the estate because in the latter year, James Lloyd junior leased from his father the Whitehouse, 69 acres and the smithy. In 1715 James junior married Mary Bartelott of Alfold, and the White-house, occupied by Abraham Pelham was settled upon them. The Pelhams were probably not a Lancing family being recorded in the registers only between 1694 and 1712, and in 1710 Abraham Pelham had married Mary Inkpen.

It is probable that the Whitehouse was enlarged at this time, and the estate passed from James to his son James, who had married Elizabeth Ann Martin. Their son James Martin Lloyd married twice. His first wife was Rebecca Green by whom he had three daughters, and of these the eldest, Rebecca Martin Lloyd survived him. He was created baronet in 1831, and his second wife was Lady Elizabeth Ann (Carr). She produced no children.

On the death of Sir James in 1844 the estate passed to his daughter Rebecca, and on her death two years later, to her step-mother Lady Elizabeth. Lady Elizabeth made her nephew Col. George Kirwen Carr her heir on the understanding that he changed his name, and in 1855 by deed poll he became Col. G. K. Carr-Lloyd. In 1877 he shot himself through the head, and the estate—now Lancing Manor passed to his son James Martin Carr-Lloyd. He was to be the last Lord of the Manor of Lancing. On his death in 1919 the estate passed to his son-in-law Col. Timothy Fetherstonhaugh. Over the next few years the lands and buildings were sold off, the manor house being sold to Lancing College who used it until 1935 as a boarding house for boys. It was pulled down in 1972, when in the ownership of Worthing Corporation.

THE LLOYD AND CARR-LLOYD FAMILY

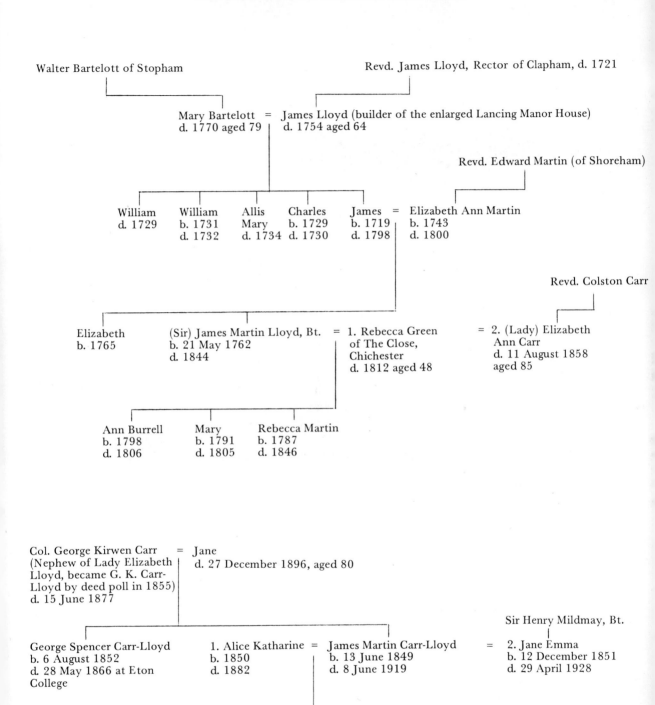

Walter Bartelott of Stopham

Revd. James Lloyd, Rector of Clapham, d. 1721

Mary Bartelott = James Lloyd (builder of the enlarged Lancing Manor House)
d. 1770 aged 79 — d. 1754 aged 64

Revd. Edward Martin (of Shoreham)

William
d. 1729

William
b. 1731
d. 1732

Allis
Mary
d. 1734

Charles
b. 1729
d. 1730

James =
b. 1719
d. 1798

Elizabeth Ann Martin
b. 1743
d. 1800

Revd. Colston Carr

Elizabeth
b. 1765

(Sir) James Martin Lloyd, Bt.
b. 21 May 1762
d. 1844

= 1. Rebecca Green
of The Close,
Chichester
d. 1812 aged 48

= 2. (Lady) Elizabeth
Ann Carr
d. 11 August 1858
aged 85

Ann Burrell
b. 1798
d. 1806

Mary
b. 1791
d. 1805

Rebecca Martin
b. 1787
d. 1846

Col. George Kirwen Carr
(Nephew of Lady Elizabeth
Lloyd, became G. K. Carr-
Lloyd by deed poll in 1855)
d. 15 June 1877

= Jane
d. 27 December 1896, aged 80

Sir Henry Mildmay, Bt.

George Spencer Carr-Lloyd
b. 6 August 1852
d. 28 May 1866 at Eton
College

1. Alice Katharine =
b. 1850
d. 1882

James Martin Carr-Lloyd
b. 13 June 1849
d. 8 June 1919

= 2. Jane Emma
b. 12 December 1851
d. 29 April 1928

Lt. Col. Timothy Fetherstonhaugh
DSO, of Kirkoswald, Cumberland

= Nancy
b. 1877
d. 11 May 1917

15. Manor Lodge, 1910. This hexagonal gatehouse was occupied by the Marshall family who were the gatekeepers for many years. The road to the right is now the A27 to Shoreham.

16. This plate shows the junction of Grinstead Lane with the Upper Brighton Road. The blue and white ice-cream tricycle (stop-me-and-buy-one) is seen passing. To the right is the wooden grocery and confectionary shop known as the 'Stormy Petrel' which was pulled down when the road was widened and developed in the 1960s.

17. The Manor cricket pavilion seen from the north and showing the bowling green. Like so many of the bungalows in Lancing, the pavilion was made from old railway carriages. It was burned down in the early 1970s and replaced by the present brick building.

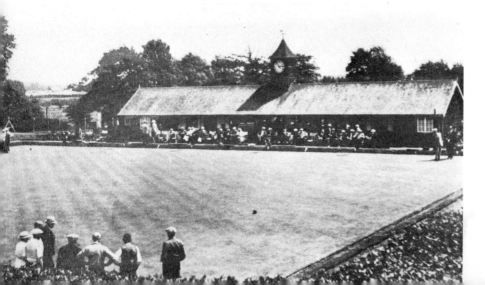

18. Malthouse Cottage is all that remains of the original Malthouse Farm, the original buildings of which appear on the 1770 map. The cottage still exists, but is hidden behind a high wall on the A27.

19. The various old buildings behind Malthouse Cottage have now been pulled down. These were probably outbuildings of Malthouse Farm.

20. Lancing Manor House looking north-east to the front facade of the building.

21. The back of the manor house looking west.

22 & 23. Lancing Manor being pulled down, 1972.

24. Manor Road showing the Corner House. This has now been pulled down and the site used as a car park for the *Sussex Potter* public house. The building was in two parts, one of which was known as Coombes Rectory since the Revd. Edward Foreman, Rector of Coombes lived there until his death in 1909, aged 80 years. The other attached house was occupied by the Hampton family.

25. Church Farm House still stands opposite the church. Early in the century it was occupied by Mrs. Wallington, sister of Mrs Carr-Lloyd, and later by Mr. and Mrs. Walpole. In 1927 Major Thomas Pemberton and his family moved into the house. It was later divided into two dwellings as at present.

26. The house known as Old Walls in Manor Road was originally called West Cottage, and was occupied in 1838 by Seth and Elizabeth Stringer until their deaths in 1868 and 1870 respectively. Seth was the gardener to Fircroft House.

27. This photograph, taken in 1908 shows the 'quain trees' which stood on each side of the gateway of Church Farm House. The boys are (*left to right*) Alf Oram, Vic Grover, Tom Boyd and Henry Steer.

28. The lower picture shows a building to the right which is now a cottage, but formerly the stables of Fircroft House.

29. Another view of the stable block of Fircroft House, now a self-contained cottage.

30. Fircroft House, formerly a private residence became a guest house, and remained as such until it was pulled down to make way for the housing estate known as Fircroft Avenue.

31. This view of Manor Road shows the farm cottages at right angles to the road. They were immediately opposite the church, and were removed in order to widen the road.

III THE OLD COTTAGE

This is probably the oldest building in Lancing; carbon dating tests having shown its timbers to be of 15th-century origin. Until recently its identity and history were obscure.

It was known that the Stringer family occupied the cottage for many years, and an examination of the census returns for 1851 and 1861 show the Stringers to be living in a house known as 'The Old Ship'. Now the 'Old Ship' was the name given to the farm house of Floods Farm, an estate of some 22 acres, and whose whereabouts were not known, but assumed to have been pulled down. Records show Floods to have adjoined Grants 'to the north' and it now seems certain that the Old Cottage is in fact Floods Farmhouse.

The farm had been sold to Judith Flood in 1641 for £200 by Sir William Goring, having been occupied before this time by her father Thomas Flood. Judith and her husband Thomas Heyward sold the farm in 1658 to Edward Jones, who in turn passed it on to his son Edward Jones junior. From Edward the farm passed to his daughter Frances Young, who lived at Grants Manor. As she had no children she left it in her will dated 1732 to her nephew John Langford, and his nephew Charles Langford sold the property to John Borrer in 1780. His son William Borrer inherited the estate in 1783 and sold it to James Lloyd in 1796. From that time until it was sold in 1920, it was part of the Lancing Manor Estate. It is now the home of Mr. and Mrs. Harry Kershaw.

32. The Old Cottage, ca. 1930.

33. The Old Cottage in 1910. The girl with the doll was Doris Grover who lived at Smithy Cottage. The boy was Stanley Whitehead, who lived at The Red House, Manor Road.

IV THE OLD FORGE AND SMITHY

A forge in Lancing is first mentioned in 1652 when 'a messuage and smith's forge with garden called Christmas in North Lancing in the occupation of Thomas Woods' was sold with other properties by Edward Hyde to Richard Streeter. In 1669 John Streeter mortgaged to John Cooke the messuage and smith's shop adjoining the orchard of Whitehouse.

In 1727 Henry Mitchener is mentioned as blacksmith, and by 1732 one George Vaughn is the smith. In 1748 Emmanuel Maxfield of Beeding bought the smithy. His wife Elizabeth Maxfield was the daughter of John Mitchener, who was a divisee under the will of Henry Mitchener, i.e. she was the grand-daughter of the last smith but one.

By 1780 the Sharp family were the owners, then the Carvers and finally the Lloyds and Carr-Lloyds. From 1866 Thomas Boniface Butler was the smith. He was followed by John Broomfield who had been his assistant. Broomfield's son Alfred worked with his father, and he was also the local chimney sweep. The Broomfields never lived in the smithy cottage (which was occupied by the Grover family) and they transferred the smithy to a barn along the Street and adjoining Shadwells. The forge was converted and became a private dwelling. John Broomfield died in 1932.

34 & 35. (*above and left*) The Old Forge after conversion to a dwelling, 1920s.

36. (*below*) The Old Forge Guest House, 1930s, now the home of Mr. and Mrs. Brian Finch.

37. (*left*) The Smithy yard. Thomas Butler on the right. From a Daguerrotype of 1870.

38. (*below*) The Smithy Cottage and the Butler family, 1890. The cottage bears the date 1728 on the west wall.

39. (*left*) Mill Road looking north, 1910. The wall to the left hides the kitchen garden of Grants Manor (seen above the wall). The upper, thatched building was a grannary later to be converted into Grannary Cottage, and pulled down in 1961. The lower building with stable doors was the smithy. It still stands and is called the Old Forge. The cart and horse belonged to the grocery company of Potter Bailey & Co. in South Street.

40. Thomas Boniface Butler, 1830 - 1900. Butler was a widower when he came to Lancing and married Clara Clapshoe, spinster, on 12 April 1856.

41. Clara Butler (Clapshoe) came from an old Lancing family. She was born on 28 April 1833 and died on 1 January 1911 aged 78 years.

42. Looking south down Mill Road, 1910. To the left is Grannary Cottage and to the right Grants Manor, at that time known as Walnut Tree Cottage. The walnut tree has long since gone, but the gap in the wall below the gate can still be seen. Until her death in 1903, the occupant of Walnut Tree Cottage had been Mrs. Charlotte Stringer, who used one room as a sweet shop. It was a favourite resort of local children and also boys from Lancing College. From 1903 until 1921 the house, still part of the Lancing Manor Estate, was let to Mr. Austin ('Ratty Austin') who spent some considerable time chasing children out of his orchards (now the site of North Lancing First and Middle School).

V GRANTS MANOR

This timber-framed house was built not later than 1540, and possibly some years earlier. Records of the Grant family are found as early as 1200 in Lancing. Various members are mentioned until the 16th century. In 1556 Grants Manor was occupied by Ralph and Alice Hacker and their son William. The property and lands were owned by Alice Hacker and it is possible that Alice could have been a Miss Grant before marriage.

At this time it seems that the manor and farm were not doing too well, and a wealthy landowner, Sir Stephen Borde of Lindfield offered to lend them money (20 Nobles, i.e. £6 13s. 4d.) on the understanding that the money should be paid back one year hence. The Hackers accepted this and signed a paper to that effect. At the appointed time for repayment, William Hacker was ill in bed and he sent in his place one John Seman (buried 23 June 1562) with the money to Lindfield. Sir Stephen Borde was not at home, and his wife refused to take the payment, saying that it was her husband's business not hers. She gave John Seman dinner and at 2 o'clock sent him back to Lancing. On the following morning Stephen Borde appeared in Lancing and pointed out that the debt had not been settled on the previous day as arranged, and that the manor now belonged to him, whereupon he took possession of the estate.

A petition was drawn up on behalf of the Hackers by Sir Thomas Palmer (builder of Parham House) and John (later Sir John) Apsley both of whom were commissioners and deputy Lieutenants of the county. The petition was sent to Queen Mary and King Philip in 1557 and later correspondence went to Queen Elizabeth in 1558. The documents recording these events have been found in the Public Record Office and although the final judgement on the case has not yet been found, the outcome is clear—the Borde family owned Grants Manor until 1623 when Stephen Borde's great grandson, Herbert Borde sold the manor to Henry Chatfield of Lancing. In 1669 Henry Chatfield's grandson Henry sold the manor to Edward Jones junior. At about this time Henry Chatfield junior had a brother Barnard, who was Headmaster of Steyning Grammar School. Edward Jones died in 1680 and his daughter Frances Young inherited the estate. An elaborate memorial to Frances Young and another to her husband are to be found on the chancel arch in the church of St. James-the-Less. They were obviously important people in the parish. The Youngs had no children, and Frances left the estate to her nephew John Langford in 1733, and in 1780 his nephew Charles Langford sold the estate to John Borrer. William Borrer, his son, sold up to James Martin Lloyd in 1796, and from that time onwards Grants was just a small part of the extensive Lancing Manor Estate.

43. (*above*) Grants Manor in 1930.

44. (*left*) Grants Manor in 1940.

45. (*right*) Part of the document concerning the disputed ownership of Grants Manor, 1557. The first two lines read: 'Deposiconds taken the viiith daie of October in the ffourth and ffyfth yeres of our sovraingn Lorde and Ladie the Kinge & Quenes maiesty before Sir Thomas Palmer knight and John Apsley comyssioners'.

46. (*left*) Grants Manor looking east towards the Tithe Barn, 1939.

47. (*below*) Mill Road in 1927. Cutting corn by hand. This site is now occupied by Norbury Drive. Boy (*left*): Sidney Ralph Wood, Mr. Burnside, Mr. Sayer and boy (*right*): John Burnside. The dog was called Pongo.

48. (*left*) The Church of England School, Mill Road in 1900. This building was erected in 1872, to the design of Richard Came, an architect living at Fircroft House. The cost of the building was £900 and this was raised by local subscription. In those early days, Miss Charlotte Tate was in charge of the infant department and Mr. William Langley was the schoolmaster in the upper school.

49. View down Mill Road in about 1938 with the beagles passing Grants Manor. During the winter, fox hounds and stag hounds would gather at Withy Patch near the *Sussex Pad* Inn at the start of the hunt and no doubt the huntsmen would fortify themselves at this hostelry before leaving!

50. The Old Tithe Barn before conversion, 1922, formerly known as Parsonage Barn. There was a pond and a saw pit close by. The barn was acquired by the McCarthay family and converted by them in 1924, under the guidance of the architect Blunden Shadbolt, into a guest house. The corrugated iron roof was removed and a thatch added. The grounds were tastefully laid out and a tennis court constructed.

The Tithe Barn underwent further exten-
n when a new set of rooms was added to
n another storey. The thatch was replaced
tiles at this time.

52 & 53. The interior of the barn was reconstructed, using old timbers and giving an ancient and mellow effect. A minstrel's gallery was built over the fireplace.

54. Mill Road leading up to the downs. The building to the left of centre, formerly the stables of Grants Manor is now Barn Elms Cottage. The cottages to the right were known as Joyces Cottages, now a single dwelling. The house in the background was built by Col.Goyder for himself, 1930. Milldene Stores now occupies the gardens of Joyces Cottages.

55. (*above*) The Street in 1910. The three cottages, formerly the homes of the Strudwick, Kimber and Saunders families have now been amalgamated into a single dwelling which has been the home of Mr. Basil Handford since 1931. These cottages together with the next one, Hawthorn Cottage, were known as Joyces Cottages, the reason for this is obscure.

VI THE STREET

56. (*left*) The horse and cart outside Hawthorn Cottage belonged to Colbourne's grocery shop, South Street. Regular deliveries were made, and the horse apparently knew exactly where to stop each time without having to be told!

57. (*below*) The Street looking east. The buildings to the left were known as Post Office Cottages. These were let to Miss Comper (postmistress), Mr. Smallwood and Mr. Phillips. The bent figure in the distance was Billy Broomfield, son of John Broomfield the blacksmith. He was a cripple, but nonetheless managed to dig the graves. ca. 1920.

58. (*top*) The Street looking west. This view shows the early victorian Baytree Cottages with Post Office Cottages beyond. Notice that the well and tree seen in the previous picture have both gone. Ca. 1939. Baytree Cottages were built on the site of a former alehouse.

59. (*above*) The house known as Shadwells stood at the east end of the Street, until the early 1960s when it was pulled down. Its outhouse seen here is still standing and is used by the Horticultural Society as a store. The last occupant of Shadwells was Mrs. Kennington, the widow of a former Lancing College Bursar. Thomas Shadwell seems to have owned property in Lancing but nowhere has the name appeared in the parish records. In Carr-Lloyd's time, Shadwells was three cottages, one occupied by the head gardener, one by the Babb family who did the laundry for the manor, and one by the cowman, Mr. Spooner.

60. (*left*) A drawing of the victorian postman at the east end of the Street. Although the houses are drawn accurately, it would not have been possible to see the windmill from this point.

VII RURAL LANCING
AND
THE DOWNS

61. (*above*) View from the downs towards Lancing College.

62. (*left*) The Chalk pit when in use, with Hill Barn and Lancing Clump.

63. (*right*) Mr. William Hurst, Lancing College shepherd with his flock in Sixteen Acre field. The Hurst family lived at Hill Barn. Hoe Court Cottages and barn can be seen in the background. The Cottage was occupied by the Bazon family.

64. View looking down Mill Road.

65. Lancing windmill when in working order. ca. 1890. The mill was last used in 1898, the miller at that time being Mr. Moseley.

66. The windmill just before being pulled down in 1905. By this time the sweeps were broken, and it was a favourite haunt of the local children who used the tailpost as a slide!

67. (*right*) Painting of the old *Sussex Pad* Inn by an unknown artist.

68. (*below*) Drawing of the old *Sussex Pad* Inn by Montague Penley. This drawing is entitled 'Near the Old Shoreham Bridge, Lancing'. Montague Penley was a Brighton artist. He always put his initials somewhere in his compositions, and in this case they are seen on the back of the small notice board. He usually included the date also, and one is tempted to wonder if the '4 severn' on the signboard indicates the date 1847 for the drawing.

69. (*right*) Remains of the old *Sussex Pad* after the fire in 1905. The present *Sussex Pad* was built on the site of the ruins in the following year.

SEAGULLS
South Lancing

70. The signal station in 1826. Coastguards were on duty continuously, wearing naval uniform and marching from the wall of the compound to the sentry box, known to the children as the bogey hut. The sentry always carried a telescope under his arm. The building to the left is the coastguard station. That in the centre is the *Three Horseshoes* Inn and to the right are the houses of The Terrace. In the far distance one can see the church of St. Nicholas at Shoreham.

VIII THE COAST

71. The coastguard cottages seen here were derelict and about to be pulled down (1955). There were two rows, the ones at the back, known as Dreadnought Cottages were for bachelors and the front row for the married men.

72. (*right*) Looking east from South Street towards Brighton shows Channel View, Beachville and The Haven in the distance.

73. (*below right*) Shops Dam is a side road leading to the beach. At one time the mouth of the river Adur opened here. Vigo Stores is now a private bungalow.

74. (*bottom*) P. C. Pateman was Lancing's only policeman in 1910. Here he is seen inspecting the remains of Tuttlebury's sweet shop after it was destroyed by fire.

75. The Grammar school, *Horseshoes* Inn and Terrace by 'J. L. D.' This drawing, made in 1900 is by an unidentified artist, 'J. L. D.' The five houses of The Terrace were built in about 1810.

76. Beach Green or Sea Green was often flooded by a high tide or a storm, the water sometimes reaching a height of three feet in the Brighton Road. This picture was taken on 16 December 1910 after a storm. The house in the centre is Mount Hermon.

77 & 78. One of the beach houses called 'Dil Khushai' seen here before (*top right*) and after (*above*) the great storm on 23 March 1913. During this storm, 54 of the wooden houses were partially or completely wrecked.

79. (*below*) Mrs. Austin (centre) was the owner of this wrecked bungalow. On the left was Mr. McCarthy, art master at Lancing College, and one of the family of photographers.

80. *Liburna*, when wrecked on the beach, was carrying a cargo of oranges, and for weeks after the wreck local children were still collecting oranges from the beach.

81. (*left*) Lancing Point, one of the more substantial beach houses.

82. (*below right*) The Round Table Cafe on the lower Brighton Road.

83. (*below*) The Brighton Road, early 1930s.

ROADS FROM LANCING

The lower road from Lancing to Worthing was built in 1808-9 but was washed away several times, leaving the upper road through north Lancing as the only route to the west.

The lower road from Lancing to Shoreham was completed in 1833 when the Norfolk Bridge was opened. Both these roads had toll gates, but with the advent of the railway between Shoreham and Worthing in 1845, the fees at the toll gates dropped, and the roads fell into a state of disrepair.

84. (*above*) Road work on the lower road to Shoreham, 1914. These men were paid 14 shillings per week as road menders.

85. (*right*) Lancing Road, or the lower road to Shoreham, when a few houses had been built, 1920s.

86. The Haven on the lower Brighton Road was quite isolated at this time. Here seen from the south, 1920.

87. The Haven just before being pulled down to make way for the block of flats, still called by the same name.

88. A view of the Widewater showing the shanty town of bungalows to the south.

89. Widewater Gardens were razed during the war in order to install anti-invasion defences. The foundations are still visible in places.

90. Salts Farm Gate Toll House.

SALTS FARM GATE TOLL HOUSE

Two toll gates were still standing in 1900, one on the Worthing Road near Ham Lane, and the other on the Shoreham Road.

A drawing by a Brighton artist—Montague Penley—shows the toll house at Salts Farm in 1841 (the date is disguised on the tariff board—IV Victoria, i.e. 1841). The name of the tollgate keeper appears to be one Sarah Gamp. Now Sarah Gamp appears as the 'nurse' in Charles Dickens' novel *Martin Chuzzlewit*, a story which was not written until 1844, at a time when Dickens was living in the Brighton area. So far Dickensian scholars have been unable to discover the origin of the name Sarah Gamp, but from this drawing it would seem quite likely that Dickens noticed the name in Lancing and incorporated it in his latest novel. A search of the parish register of Lancing and Shoreham has failed to reveal this name, but one Sarah Hills (nee Cramp) gave birth to children in 1835, 1838 and 1840. The address of the couple is given as Lancing Station House (i.e. Coastguards Station—there was no railway at that time) not far from the toll house. Could Dickens have seen 'Sarah Cramp' and altered it to Sarah Gamp?—or indeed is it 'Sarah Gamp' on the drawing?

Sarah Hills (Cramp) died in 1869, aged 71 and John died in 1868 aged 74 years.

IX (i) LANCING'S CONVALESCENT HOMES

The southern convalescent homes were first established in Lancing in June 1890. They were started, in a very modest way, as an auxiliary to the Kingsland (North-East London) Gospel mission, by Mr. William Chorley. Having worked for many years with the poor in London, he realised that a change of scenery and a breath of fresh sea air would improve the physical and spiritual well-being of people from that city's depressed areas.

In 1889, a Mr. Northcroft offered the use of his house, 'Bank Cottage', to Mr. Chorley, rent free, for the summer months. This modest red-brick house still stands on the corner of South Street just below the *Three Horseshoes* Inn. The limited accommodation provided a holiday for ten children at any one time, and proved to be a great success.

In the following year the old Grammar school building, which had been closed for some time, came onto the market and it was purchased by a Mr. Wenman. The new owner was at once approached by Mr. Chorley who persuaded Mr. Wenman to grant him the free use of the house for 21 years. It was named The Maria Wenman Home of Rest, in memory of the owner's deceased wife. Classrooms were converted to bedrooms and dayrooms, and the kitchen and dining room renovated. The dining hall doubled as a mission hall where regular Sunday services were held, to which the local people were welcome. Within three months of opening, no less than 450 patients had been received. The home soon became known as 'The Chestnuts', not from the trees which stood in its grounds (they were *Ilex*), but from the fact that many of the inmates suffered from chest complaints.

The buildings were extended, the first new wing opening in 1901, and a new mission room was in use by 1903.

Mr. Chorley had long wanted a home for men so that they might accompany their wives and children and, as luck would have it, a house on the opposite side of South Street, known as 'Lorne Cottage' became vacant in 1895 and it was opened in the same year as a rest home for 10 men. This again soon became inadequate for its purpose and in 1899 a house facing the sea and known as the 'Stork's Nest' was acquired, renamed 'Channel View', and opened for 30 men and youths. The inmates of 'Channel View' wore a uniform of rough navy-blue serge and were known to the villagers as 'Chorley's Blue Birds'. After Lorne Cottage had been vacated by the men, it was used to house a few aged women so that they might end their days in peace and comfort. The alternative for many of them would have been the dreaded workhouse. In 1907 a new house, known as 'Mount Hermon', was built to house the permanent residents and 'Lorne Cottage' became the home and studio of the McCarthy family. In order to segregate women with babies from the rest, Mr. Chorley bought the house next door, known as 'Hope Lodge' in 1896 for £425. This provided accommodation for 12 or more mothers and their babies.

In 1912 the large house next door to 'Channel View' was acquired and opened as 'Beachville' Home for men. This was eventually taken over by the W.S.C.C. as a home for old people and is still in existence, taking about forty residents. It has subsequently been renamed 'Sussex Lodge'.

In 1928 Mr. William Chorley retired as secretary of the convalescent homes, and his place was taken by his son, Henry. In this same year, the Bell Memorial Home for convalescent women was opened on the site to the north of 'Hope Lodge' which, together with the old 'Chestnuts' building, was demolished. Since that time things have remained almost unchanged to the present day.

During the 1939-45 war the Homes were requisitioned for use as emergency hospitals, and occupied by units from the Canadian army. Part of the Home was bombed and subsequently rebuilt.

Mr. and Mrs. Chorley lived in a house named 'Cromehurst', one of a group of houses built in about 1810 and known as the Terrace. He died on 22 November 1932, aged 84 and Mrs. Chorley survived him by only three months and died in March 1933. They are buried in the West Lain part of North Lancing cemetery.

91. (*left*) Mount Hermon built in 1907.

92. (*lower left*) Lancing Grammar School, ca. 1860.

93. (*below*) The dining room of the former Grammar School was also used for the same purpose after it became the Chestnuts.

94. (*above*) The Chestnuts rest home.

95. (*right*) Mr. Chorley, born 1848, died 1932 aged 84 years.

96. The Chestnuts. View from the *Three Horseshoes* Inn.

Homes of Rest Lancing From the Beach

97. (*above*) Homes of rest from the beach, 1920s.

98. (*left*) Mrs. Chorley in the early 1930s.

99. (*below*) Channel view, formerly the Stork's Nest.

CHANNEL VIEW. LANCING.

100. Beachville.

101. The dining room at Beachville. This house is still standing,
and is now called Sussex Lodge.

102. Sunbeam and Bell memorial homes, 1939.

103. (*above*) Convalescent homes after bombing during the early part of the war.

104. (*below left*) The Children's Heart Home. This was later replaced by flats, now known as Warren Court, Sompting Road.

105. (*below right*) Miss Booker, founder and Matron of the homes, 1926-1948.

IX (ii) THE WARREN HEART HOME

In 1927, Miss Maud A. Booker and her friend Miss A. Newton opened what had previously been a preparatory school, as a convalescent home for children and babies. They had a similar home at Kingsnorth near Ashford, Kent, but were in need of larger premises when 'The Warren' became available.

In 1930, at the request of the Great Ormond Street Hospital for Sick Children, Miss Booker used her Home to concentrate on children suffering from rheumatic heart disease. At that time there were 30 patients and a nursing staff of ten. In the following year, as a result of substantial grants received from the Peter Pan Fund, established by Sir James Barrie, considerable extensions were made and three years later, in 1934, a schoolroom, dining room and Bluebell Ward were opened. By this time there were 76 patients, and the home was renamed the Maud Booker Heart Home as a tribute to the founder.

In 1937, a nurses' home was built, but when the war started Lancing became a restricted area, and on the 22 August 1940, the home was evacuated to Cuckfield. They returned to Lancing on 27 March 1945, and in July 1948 the Home was taken over by the new National Health Service. The Ministry of Health decided that it was too costly to run, the patients were transferred to Carshalton, and the Home finally closed in 1950. Miss Newton died on 28 May 1952. Miss Booker was cared for as a resident at the Bell Memorial Home until her death in August 1967.

106. Mr. Cass was a grocer and baker in South Street. He was also the miller at this time, grinding the corn on the downs, and baking the bread here in South Street. Hope Lodge can be seen to the right. Cass's shop later became Potter Bailey & Co. of Worthing, and finally A. J. Smith Provisions.

X SOUTH STREET

107. Hope Lodge and the *Three Horseshoes* Hotel.

108. Ivy Cottages in East Street. These are still standing

109. South Street with East Street to the right, 1900.

110. These two cottages backing onto Ivy Cottages in East Street have now been pulled down. There were two steps leading up to the front door of the taller cottage, known as Step House, and possibly the site of the original *Three Horseshoes* Inn.

111. (*below*) Trevetts bread van, the first mechanical commercial vehicle in Lancing.

12. Trevetts shop at the corner of Alma Street, where sweets and tobacco were sold.

13. (*below left*) Lovegrove's shop, tailor and outfitter. This later became Aston's the Chemist.

14. (*right*) Martin Fuller the greengrocer and fruiterer was the son of Martin Fuller senior, market gardener of Violet Cottage. Martin junior's son, Stanley, seen here died at an early age from appendicitis.

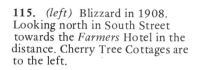

115. *(left)* Blizzard in 1908. Looking north in South Street towards the *Farmers* Hotel in the distance. Cherry Tree Cottages are to the left.

116. *(centre left)* Blizzard in 1908. Looking towards the site of the future Parish Hall.

117. *(bottom)* Chesham Terrace and P.C. Pearce, 1912.

118. (*right*) Bushby's Homestead with fig trees. This was on the site of the present Chesham House. The Bushby's are an old Lancing family, first recorded in the parish in 1566.

119. (*centre right*) Church Parade, 1912. Passing the site of the present Parish Hall, before St. Michael's Church was built.

120. (*bottom*) The same site some years later after the Parish Hall had been built. A reading room, now St. Michael's Church Hall was built for the Parish Council, but was also used by the Church Lads Brigade, by the Sunday School and for evening classes in woodwork, pottery, drawing and painting.

121. (*right*) Tom Luckin the butcher. Later the butcher's shop was taken over by Hodsons.

122. (*below*) Colbourne's Shops. This block was known as Commerce House. One of the shops was run by Arthur Colbourne the grocer, and next door, Walter Colbourne, his brother, ran a draper's shop.

123. (*left*) Yew Tree Cottages stood opposite the end of Penhill Road, on the site of the present block of flats.

124. (*right*) Yew Tree Cottages on fire, 1955.

125. (*below*) Firemen at Yew Tree Cottages. At the time of the fire, all but one of the cottages were empty.

126. (*left*) Wesleyan Chapel, now the Methodist Church, built in 1910.

127. (*below*) Wesleyan Sunday School outing, 1910.

128. (*right*) The old *Farmers* Hotel.
The gardens of Pond Row can be seen
to the right. Alongside the *Farmers*
Hotel was the Drill Hall. This was used
for political meetings, concerts, band
practice etc.

129. (*below*) Salt Lake in 1912 where
some of the houses are still standing.

30. (*right*) 'Picturesque Cottages'.
hese Cottages dating back to the 17th
entury were in a dilapidated condition
hen pulled down in 1926. They were
pposite the *Farmers* Hotel and next to
iolet Cottage, ca. 1915.

Old Thatched Cottages, Lancing.

131. (*above*) Myrtle Cottages 1907. Mrs. Emsley with her daughters Dorothy (1896-1908) and Winifred Edith (b. 1892).

132. (*left*) These 'Old Thatched Cottages' were in fact built in 1926 to replace the earlier ones.

133. (*below left*) These cottages, built in 1926 were in turn pulled down in the 1960s to make way for a row of shops opposite the *Farmers* Hotel.

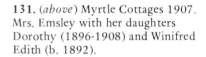

134. View from Pond Row towards Elm Grove. Violet Cottage to the right centre and *Farmers* Hotel on the extreme right. The house in Elm Grove was the home of Dr. Prentice, Lancing's first resident physician.

135. Violet Cottage, home of the Fuller family.

136. Station Road leading from the *Farmers* Hotel to the station. The *Luxor* now stands on this site. The Barber's shop, Searles, (with pole) was formerly Evershed's dairy.

137. Lancing near Worthing.

138. Bicycles at the crossing.

139. (*left*) Level crossing showing the signal box in its original site. The old man with the cart is Mr. Robert Bartlett, who was both station-master and postmaster.

140. (*centre*) Roberts Road at the turn of the century.

141. (*bottom right*) Cecil Road at the turn of the century.

142.   Page and Stanbrook Bakeries, Penhill Road. Penhill Road was first opened in 1887 as Jubilee Road.

143.   A. G. Page horse and cart. The bakery in Penhill Road was started by two men who originally worked for Potter Bailey & Co., Messrs. Page and Stanbrook. Mr. Stanbrook later left the partnership to set up a business on his own, but died soon afterwards. The shop then became the property of Alick Page.

144. Lancing railway station in 1900. The roads were unmetalled and very muddy.

145. The railway crossing with horse and cart in 1910. The *Railway* Hotel (now the *Merry Monk*) in the background.

146. (*above*) Lancing station and porters, 1907.

147. (*centre*) Bungalow Town Halt, 1932/33. This station, which was at the point where the road runs under the track near Shoreham Airport, was opened in 1910 as Bungalow Town Halt. It was closed in 1933, but opened again two years later as Shoreham Airport Station, and was finally closed in 1940. The line was electrified in 1932 and hence the date of the picture must be 1932-33.

148. (*below left*) Shoreham Airport, 16 March 1911.

9. North Road Shops. These were butcher, grocer, shoemaker and post office.

50. Post office with postmen, 1912. (*left to right*) Tom Greet, Henry Puttick, George Humphrey and Robert Bartlett, the postmaster.

151. Shops with Culverhouse, 1950.

152. Culverhouse, 1920. Culverhouse, with its Horsham stone roof was probably an Elizabethan building. A reference in the Parish Register shows that John Swift, son of John, living at Culverhouse was baptized in 1650. It was a guest house at the time of its destruction in the 1960s.

153. North Road Cottages and Almshouses, 1907. The girls in the picture are Eadie Green, May Merriott and Olive Cooper who is holding Bessie Oram.

154. North Road. The houses to the left formed part of a close known as Little Croft. The houses to the right are still in use as a solicitor's office.

North Road Lancing.

155. Little Croft. This site is now the Queensway shops and car park.

156. North Road looking north. The houses to the left have been replaced by the Keymarket shopping parade.

157. North Road looking south, 1930. The tall chimneys on the left are the Penfold Almshouses.

158. North Road looking south.

159. (*right*) Laurel Lodge, North Road.

160. Elm Trees in North Road, 1900. Monks Farm can be seen in the background. The Police Station now stands on the site of the left hand hedge.

161. Shops and bus in North Road. The bus is standing by the wall of Fürst Haus, now Woolworths.

162. (*left*) Monks Farm and cottages. Addison Square now occupies the foreground.

163. (*bottom left*) Grinstead Lane. The Grinstead family were farmers at New Salts Farm, being represented in the parish register between 1779 and 1862. Grinstead Lane leads from Capers Lane (now Crabtree Lane) to the manor and Upper Brighton Road. It was originally the only vehicular approach to North Lancing and Shoreham from South Lancing. At the corner of Grinstead Lane and Capers Lane was a walled square of land known as the Pound and used to accommodate stray cattle.

164. Church Path leading from South to North Lancing, now called First Avenue.

165. (*above & right*) Pullenbury's Cottages in Grinstead Lane. These cottages, built in 1896 were sometimes known as Burry's Cottages, or Malthouse Cottages. The photograph was taken in 1907 when they were occupied by the Monnery, Hibdidge, Till and Jenkins families. The children (*left to right*): Gertie Hibdidge, Hilda Hibdidge, Eva Till and Albert Jenkins.

166. (*above*) Cokeham Manor, now gone, used to lie to the west of the parish of Lancing.

167. (*left*) Boundstone Lane, so called from the boundary stone dividing the parish of Lancing from that of Sompting. The boundary stone is now preserved and mounted for display at Boundstone School.

RESIDENTS
of Lancing

XII LANCING SCHOOLS

There were several private schools in Lancing, one of the earliest being Lancing Grammar School, a boarding school for about 150 boys. This dated back to the early 19th century, but was closed in about 1880 and was later to become the 'Chestnuts' Convalescent Home.

Miss Bunting opened Lancing Preparatory School, which catered for boys aged four to eight and girls up to the age of 10 years. It was held in the Methodist Hall, ideally suited for this purpose, as it could be divided by partitions into smaller rooms. The school was sold to Miss McCarthy, sister of the photographer, who ran it for some years before selling to Mrs. Heyman. She owned the establishment for two years, then sold it to Miss Phyllis Perry (now Mrs. Denman). Miss Perry had charge of the school from 1933 to 1948, and at this time most of its pupils went on to Shoreham Grammar School or the girls to Worthing. Miss Perry passed the school on to Mrs. Rees, and it closed down soon afterwards.

A similar school for girls and small boys, known as 'Viking House' School was run by Mrs. Old in Kings Road, and also 'The Warren' in Sompting Road had been a private school for boys before it became a nursing home for children.

The National School in Mill Road, meant to cater for 150 children, was erected in 1872 at a cost of £900 which had been raised by local subscription. William Langley was the schoolmaster, with Miss Tate in charge of the infants department. By 1890 William John Marriott had become the schoolmaster and when he died in 1903 his widow Anne Marriott continued for some time in charge of the school. Mr. Walter Giles Heaton joined the staff soon afterwards and remained headmaster until 1916 when he left to join the army.

By 1900 a new classroom had to be built as there were 180 children on roll. The population of Lancing stood at about 800 and there were 194 houses in the parish. Miss Daisey Humphrey joined the staff in 1914 and on the departure of Mr. Heaton became Headmistress, which she remained until her retirement in 1954.

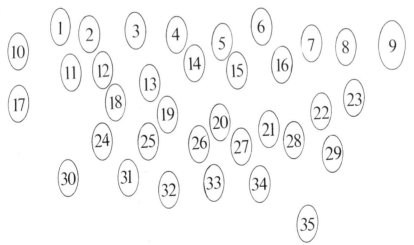

168. Lancing School, ca. 1892.

1. Bill Saunders
2. Edwin Fuller
3. Leo Prideaux
4. Unidentified
5. - Dowker
6. Bartley Grover
7. Clem Russell
8. Harry Best
9. Mr. W. J. Marriott
10. Lilian Saunders
11. Unidentified
12. Annie Broomfield

13. Nelly Grover
14. A. Marriott
15. Unidentified
16. Fanny Russell
17. Unidentified
18. May Russell
19. G. Marriott
20. Unidentified
21. Ernie Barnett
22. George Barnett
23. Frank Lisher
24. May Trevett

25. May Lisher (Mrs. Bushby)
26. Unidentified
27. - Savage
28. Unidentified
29. Laddie Trevett
30. George Lisher
31. Ivy Butler
32. Bessie Trevett
33. Lily Best
34. Jessie Prideaux
35. Unidentified

169. William John Marriott, died 28 February 1903.

170. Mrs. Martha Ann Marriott, died 20 January 1918.

171. Miss Charlotte Tate's Class, 1901. Back row: Miss Tate, (?), Nellie Oldham, Tom Prideaux, Arthur Nutley, Will Hurst, Arthur Parker, (?), Louisa Lyons, Miss Alice Saunders; third row: (?), (?), (?), Ella Bates, Sally Slaughter, Violet Hurst, (?), Annie Richardson; second row: (?), (?), Enid Rossiter, Billy Babb, Meggie Steer, George Hurst, (?), (?); front row: (?), (?), (?), Mable Ives, (?), (?), (?), Gert Cager.

172. Mr. Heaton's Class, 1908. Back row: Mr. W. G. Heaton, Phyllis Horton, Emily Lower, Alma Trevett, Hilda Richardson, Dorothy Bolt; third row: Fred Charles, May Merriott, Bernard Peters, Maggie Gammons, Martin Snelling, Gertrude Hibdige; second row: Alice Bashford, Gay Hurst, Lizzie Tasker, Selina Sharp, Grace Comper, Doris Grover, Barbara Trevett; front row: Bernard Lelliott, Leonard Heaton, George Heaton, Archie Colbourne.

173. Mr. Heaton's Garden Class, 1908. Back row: Mr. Heaton, Martin Snelling, Vic Grover, Basil Marshall, Bill Self, Fred Charles; third row: Fred Cherrills, Tom Trevett, Bill Trevett, Tom Boyd, Bernie James; second row: Ralph Piper, Stan Whitehead, Ralph Curd, Arthur Howard, Bernie Peters, Alf Pelling; front row: Archie Colbourne, Bernie Lelliott.

174. Mrs. Marriott's Class, 1907. Back row: Mrs. Anne Marriott, Archie Colbourne, Ted Feldwick, Bernie Peters, Martin Snelling, Ralph Piper, Edison Penfold, Clifford Penfold, Horace Best, Henry Steer, Will Dann; second row: Eric Colbourne, Kathie Colbourne, Kathie Page, Fred Fuller, Baden Luckin, Stan Fuller, Steve Stringer, Bertram Colbourne, Percy Douglas, Reg Best, John Dann, Hubert Curd (standing in front); front row (seated): Olive Colbourne, Barbara Trevett, George Searle, Fred Charles, Syd Page, Mable Page, Ruby Piper, Hildred Piper.

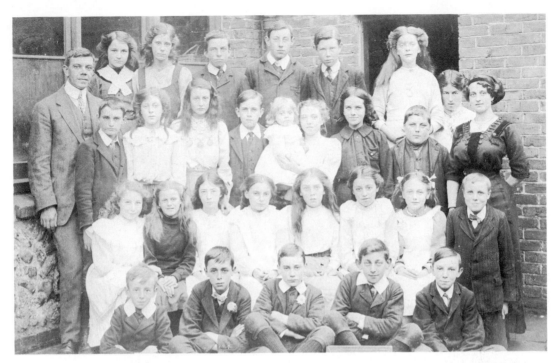

175. Lancing School, 1913. Back row: Mr. Heaton, Eadie Parker, Eadie Aldridge, Walter Saddler, Bill Dann, Fred Marshall, Adelaide Wiltshire, Olive Colbourne; third row: (?), Kathleen Page, Annie Young, Reg Page, Beryl Heaton, Eva Till, Hilda Hibdidge, Ted Page, Mrs. Stone; second row: Chrisie Lisher, Elsie Page, Frances Stevens, Ivy Lower, Kathie Greet, Grace Bazon, Ruby Piper, Les Cousins; front row: Cliff Kenward, Stan Fuller, Frank Scott, John Dann, Harry Potter.

176. Mr. Heaton's Garden Class, 1914. Back: Mr. Heaton; back row: Reg Stilwell, Bert Lisher, second row: Horace Best, Harry Potter, Syd Page, Eric Colbourne, Ted Page, Reg Page; front row: Frank Stevens, Tom Searle, Jasper Trevett, Clifford Penfold.

177. Lancing School, 1919, Group B. Back row: Olive Page, Olive White, Edna Trevett, (?), George James Kimber; third row: Martin Pearce, Stan Herbert, Ted Othen, William Tim Webber, George Sharp; second row: Lilian Thorns, Arthur Kimber, Dorothy Sharp, Reg Page, (?), Gladys Page; front row: Alick Page, Will Harman, (?), Dorothy McLellan.

178. Lancing School Teachers, 1919. Miss Boxhall, Mrs. Heaton, Miss Humphrey, Miss Heaver; seated: Miss Walker.

179. Lancing School, 1920, Group 5. Back row: Dick Chatfield, Bob Upfield, Lorna Holland, Eadie Millard, Carrie Cozens, Bill Holland; middle row (standing): May Warr, Denzil Battrick, Percy Strudwick, George Millard, Ted Chatfield, Archie Cozens, Dolly Howard; front row: Gert Strudwick, Gladys Cozens, Reg Green, Bob Green, Joan Warr; sitting on ground: Roland Croucher, Bertha Howard, Gilbert Battrick.

180. Lancing School, 1920, Group 7. Back row: (?), Stella Steer, (?), (?), Laura Matten, (?), middle row: Gilbert Howard, John Howard, Alfie Sievier, Eddie Gregory, Leo Matten, Bill Nicholls; front row: Vicky Pelling, Gladys Meads, Alec Matten, Nancy Fuller, Ethel 'Birdie' Howard.

181. Lancing School, 1921, Group 4. Back row: (?), Nellie Minter, 'Joker' Rose, Harry Cox, Bert Johns; third row: May Benn (Mrs. Charman), Janet Puttick, George Bushby, Irene Hayes, Dorothy Marchant, George Fuller, Jim 'Jumbo' Kimber; second row: Beryl Heaton, Marion Cooper, Jessie Goodyer, Lil Sharp, Ben Pescod; front row: (?), (?), Emily Wood, George Prideaux, (?) Annie Norris (Mrs. Roy Marshall).

182. Lancing School Football Team, 1921. (South Downs School League. Founder: Major Sexton). Back row: Miss D. Humphrey, Mr. C. Potter, Mr. F. Hall, Mr. Jack Harber; third row: Syd Haylor, Jack Colman, Les Tingley; second row: Bob Green, Bill Harman, Dick Saunders, George Harber, Dick Perry; front row: Charlie Potter, 'Dids' Hall, Alf Hall.

183. Empire Day. North Lancing School, 1924.

184. Miss Bunting's Private School. Back row: Gladys McCarthy, Winnie Roberts, Syd Bates, Donald Hoppet, Miss Bunting, Eileen Leech, Ted Roberts, Albert 'Dimple' Badcock; middle row: Nora Gammons, Harold Russell, - Raven, Dorothy Harman, May Perham, Alice Young, (?), (?); front row: Colin Gammans, Reg Page, (?), Cecil Gammans, Molly Haque, Dorothy Sharp.

185. South Lancing School, 1914. Teachers: Miss Bessie Trevett, **Mrs. Curd** (Miss Stewart); Back row: (?), Percy Strudwick, (?), Les Tingley, N. Sharp, Stanley Harbutt, Charlie Potter, (?), Arthur Weaver; middle row: Harrold Craddock, (?), Edgar Young, Eileen Page, May Dean, Carrie Cozens, Marion Cooper; front row: (?), 'Buck' Chatfield, (?), Tom Harber, Gilbert Howard, Albert Dean.

186. South Lancing School, 1923. Back row: (?), (?), Joe Prideaux, (?), John Brown, (?), Peter Pescod, Robin Nicholls; front row: Joan Prideaux, Molly Strudwick, Barbara Mitchell, Georgina Steer, (?), Evelyn Lisher, (?).

XIII LANCING COLLEGE

Lancing College was founded by the Revd. Nathaniel Woodard, curate of St. Mary's, Shoreham. He was distressed by the lack of education among the poorer classes, and he resolved to establish a grammar school where instruction could be given in navigation, French and the elements of religion. A day school was started in the dining room of the vicarage in Shoreham, and this was to grow into St. Mary's School, with fees of £5 per annum.

The success of St. Mary's School encouraged Woodard to enlarge his horizon and he proposed the founding of a federation of boarding schools for all classes of society. Although he was without financial means, Woodard managed to persuade many important, influential and wealthy people including Lord Salisbury, Gladstone and Henry Tritton to part with large sums of money, and in 1858 the college of SS. Mary and Nicholas was able to move into its new premises in Lancing. His two other schools, at Hurstpierpoint and Ardingly were by now established.

All Woodard schools are based on the teaching of the Christian religion according to the doctrines of the Church of England, and this was to be the focal point of all teaching. 'Education without religion is a pure evil' said Woodard. A special feature was the great chapel at Lancing, built as a central minster for all the schools in the federation to meet together from time to time.

Since those early days, the founding of schools within the corporation has continued and there are now some twenty-six Woodard schools.

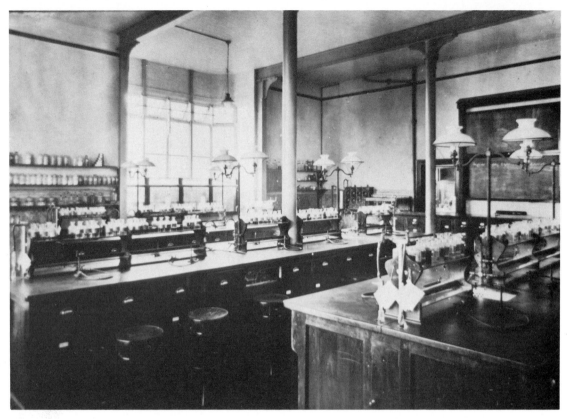

187. Chemistry Laboratory. The science laboratories were built in 1908 and consisted of one chemistry, one physics and one biology laboratory together with two preparation rooms and a lecture theatre. Since those days, the department has increased and now has twelve laboratories.

188. The swimming pool. The bath was excavated, using boy labour, and constructed by the college workmen in 1904. The total cost involved was two thousand pounds. This pool will close at Easter 1982 when it will be replaced by a new pool.

189. Lower Dining Hall, built 1857. This crypt to the dining hall was first used as a breakfast room and later became the Armoury. In 1959 it was divided into two rooms, a smaller armoury and a masters' dining room.

190. The Upper Dining Hall, completed in 1867. The magnificent dining hall is 101 ft. long, 38 ft. wide and 70 ft. high. At the south end is the high table and at the north end is the ante-hall with a gallery over it. The amorial stained glass in the windows must be some of the finest in the country.

191. (*above*) Fields House with Olds House to the right. Fields House, which was completed in 1912 is, like the rest of the main building, made of flint with Caen stone dressings. The house was named after Lancing's first chaplain.

193. (*below*) The Chapel of Lancing College under construction, 1885. At this time only the first section of the roof had been built, and the clerestory windows were still being erected.

194. (*opposite top*) Lancing College Chapel in 1893. At this stage, the roof had still to be completed together with the west wall. Woodard, who died in 1891 lived long enough to see most of his chapel built.

195. (*opposite below left*). Chapel Nave completed, 1908. The shell of the chapel was now complete, and the floor about to be paved with Portland stone which had been salvaged from a wreck off Shoreham. The stone had been destined for new Home Office buildings in Westminster.

192. (*above*) The Old Farm House and College Pond, ca. 1877. This Elizabethan house, originally called Burwells Farm, has, since this photograph was taken, been extended and has for many years been the residence for the Headmaster of Lancing College. The chapel can be seen in the distance, built up to the level of the aisle windows.

196. The Revd. Edmund 'Mugs' Field M. A.
Lancing's first chaplain, a post which he held
for 37 years from 1854. Field was a saintly man
who devoted his life to Lancing. He was a great
nephew of Gilbert White of Selbourne. After
his retirement he continued to live at Lancing
College, and died there in 1901.

197. (*left*) Boys in Addison Square, 1908. (*left to right*): Tom Boyd, George Fairs, Bill Stanley, Vincent Peters, Ted Feldwick (front) and Tom Trevett.

198. (*below*) Alexander and Daisey Boyd, 1886. Alexander Boyd, father of Tom above, was a coast-guard (Coastguard Station in the background). He was born in 1846 and died in 1911 aged 65. His daughter Daisey, was born in 1883 and died in 1978 aged 95, as Mrs. Guyatt.

199. The Merriott family, 1900. Standing: Jim, Ellen (Mrs. Warr); seated: May (Mrs. White), Ted, Mrs. Merriott and Bert (Dodger) Merriott. Mr. Merriott was the gardener and Mrs. Merriott the nurse to the Ricardo family at Penstone House.

200. (*right*) Penstone Park Hotel shortly before being pulled down to make way for the Health Centre and Library.

201. (*below*) Penstone House, north side.

202. (*below*) Penstone House, south side; the home of Sir Harry Ricardo and family. (*left to right*): Kate, Angela, Lady Ricardo and Camilla.

203.   Interior of Penstone House: the drawing room.

204.   Sir Harry's workshop.

205. Womens Institute play. (*left to right*): Mrs. Kate Matten, (?), Olive Lisher (Mrs. Page), Bessie Lisher (Mrs. Killock).

206. Sunday School outing to the beach, 1922.

207. (*above*) The Finches, home of the Lishers. This house in Elm Grove was pulled down and rebuilt in 1927.

208. (*top right*) Four generations of Lishers. George, born 1840, his son George born 1857, his son George born 1887 and his son George born 1914.

209. Alick Page, Penhill Bakery, 1938.

210. The wedding of Mr. and Mrs. George White, 1902.

211. Lancing Parish Council on the lawn at Lancing Manor, 1910.

212. (*above*) Archibald Colbourne who was the son of Walter Colbourne, draper of Commerce House, born 2 November 1897, died 1980. The photograph was taken in 1917.

213. (*left*) P.C. Pearce of Lancing, 1912.

214. Church Farm House and the Pemberton family, 1930. (*left to right*): Mrs. Ethel Pemberton, Mrs. Lilian Pemberton (sister-in-law), Jane, Busick, Margaret and Major Thomas Pemberton. Jane and Margaret are daughters of Thomas and Ethel Pemberton and Busick is the son of Roger and Lilian Pemberton. The Pembertons were at Church Farm House from 1927 to 1953.

XV SPORTS AND PASTIMES

From the turn of the century, football and cricket were played at Sea Green; and later by permission of J. M. Carr-Lloyd, Lord of the Manor, in the manor grounds and on the vicarage glebe.

215. Lancing Football Team, 1915-1916. Back row: (*left to right*): Arthur Howard, George Barnett, Bert Howard, Gordon Barrett, Ted Monnery, Bert Merriott; middle row: Bernie Peters, Frank Gammon, Ted Saunders ?; front row: Frank Badcock, Len Parker, Ophir Keating, Edwin Norris, (?).

216. Lancing Football Team, 1918. Back row: Bert (Dodger) Merriott, Charlie Day, Harold Carter, Jesse McKeon, Wally Wakeham, Fred Peters, Arthur Howard; middle row: Ernest Payne, Joe Strotten, George Turner; front row: Syd Field, Tom Steel, Bernie Peters, Gordon Barrett, Len Parker, Jim Merriott.

217. Lancing United Football Club, 1921-22. Back row (*left to right*): Bert Merriott, Henry Burstow, Joe Strotten, Len Lawrence, Alick Battrick, Ben Steer; middle row: Bill Scrace, Fred Battrick, Fred Peters; front row: Rupert Battrick, Buller Battrick, Gordon Barrett, Ted Edwards, Ted Monnery.

218. Lancing United Football Club and Mascot, 1923-24. Back row (*left to right*): Henry (?) Burstow, Jim Wood, Joe Strotten, - Green, Alick Battrick, Ted Monnery, George Barnett, (? - hat), Charlie Richardson; middle row: Bim Ireland, Drummer Duke, Frank Gammons, Rupert Battrick, Bill Scrace, Fred Battrick (hat); front row: Alick Tompkins, George Turner.

219. Lancing Cricket Team about 1890. Standing (*left to right*): Tom Butler, E. Marshall, Hartley Smith, (?), F. Grover snr, C. Barber snr; middle row, standing: C. Comper, F. Fuller, - Burtenshaw, J. Greenyear, J. Russell snr; seated: T. Peters, H. Peters, A. Steel, A. Robins, F. Kennard.

220. Lancing Cricket Club, 1909. Standing: Ted Monnery, George Barnett, Jack Weaver, Bert Lisher, Ted Saunders, George Lisher, Syd Saunders, Percy Marshall, Reg Saunders, Mr. Easter, Frank Fuller; seated: Charlie Comper, Bartley Grover, Frank Lisher, Bill Saunders and lying on the ground: George Fairs.

221. Lancing Cricket Club, 1920. Standing (*left to right*): Jim Merriott, George White (secretary), Jack Payne, Ted Monnery, Ernie Barnett, Will Saunders, Frank Lisher, George Lisher; sitting: George Fairs, Arthur Grover, Syd Saunders, Bart Grover, Hubert Lisher. The three Lishers were brothers, as were the two Grovers. The two Saunders were cousins.

222. Lancing Cricket Team, 1922. Standing (*left to right*): Jim Lisher, Charlie White, Ernie Barnett, Bartley Grover, Albert (Dimple) Badcock, Alf Jacks, Ted Othen, George White; middle row: Ted Monnery, Jack Payne, Bill Saunders, Cecil Thomas, Reg Cass; front row: Syd Saunders, Buller Battrick.

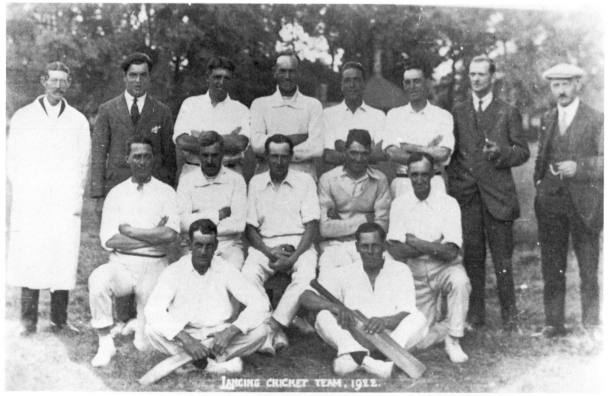

223. Cricket Tea at Lancing Manor. A cricket tea was provided by the Carr-Lloyd family each year in 'The Park' as the Manor grounds were known.

224. Lancing Cricket Team, 1924. 2nd XI. Standing: Arthur Aldridge, Bill Latter, Frank Elliott, George Lisher, Ben Steer, Ron Grover, Charlie White; seated: Wally Wakeham, Bim Ireland, Buller Battrick, Frank Lisher, Tim Webber.

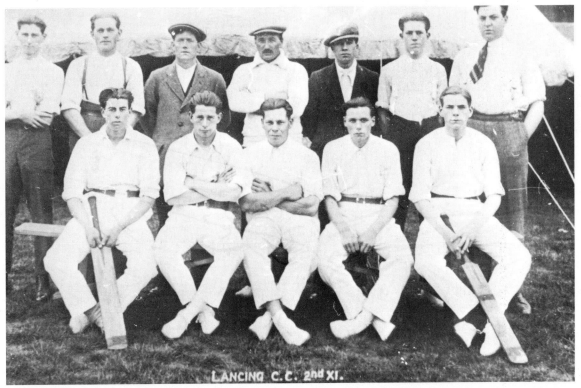

225. (*above*) Lancing Quoits Club, 1907. Standing (*left to right*): Eli Warr, Harry Fakenbridge, (?), Charlie Matten, Billy Babb, George Haller, Edwin Fuller, Mark Fuller; sitting: Tom Till, Cephas Gammans, George Humphrey, Charlie Humphrey, Sam Warr.

226. (*below*) Quoits Club in action. Quoits was played in the brickfields off Penhill Road.

227. *(above)* Boys Brigade Camp at Steyning, 1910. Standing back row *(left to right):* Bernie Peters, Reg Lisher, Horace Strudwick, Vincent Peters, George Nutley, George Hurst, Nat Blacker, Fred Collins, Len Parker, Martin Snelling Jack Nutley, Basil Marshall; front row: Bert Merriot, Stan Collins, Hector Boyd, Vic Grover, Tom Boyd, Revd. Peel, Capt. Georg Cass, Sgnt. Percy Blacker, Arthur Howard, Tom Trevett, Arthur Bartlett, Bill Trevett, Goerge Fairs.

228. *(opposite below)* Funeral of Walter Stenning, 1910. Walter Stenning (born 7 July 1895) worked as an apprentice gardener after leaving school at the age of 14. A keen member of the Boys Brigade, he died from lockjaw after accidentally sticking a garden fork through his foot.

229. *(right)* Boys Brigade leaders. Back row: Tom Boyd, Vic Grover, Horace Strudwick, front row: Bert Merriott, Capt. G. Cass, Percy Blaker, Vincent Peters. Captain George Cass was the son of James Cass, farmer of Culverhouse Farm. He was a bachelor and ran the Boys Brigade and also started the Scout Troop. He was church organist and choir master after the departure of Mr. Walter Heaton.

230. (*above*) Lancing Band, 1918-20.

231 & **232.** (*right & below*) Scout Troop, 1909.

233. Comic football match, 1920s. Back row (*left to right*): Mr. Aitken, Fred Redman, Bart Grover, Reg Page, Frank Lisher, Dave Urrey; second row: Mr. Pycroft, Frank Badcock, (?), Bill Hyde, Harry Pearce, Jim Souter, Alick Page; third row: Mr. Deeping, (?), Mr. Tonken, R. Hawkins, Bernie Hodson, Mr. West; front row: H. Symons, Fred Marshall, Hawkins junior, Les Nairn, (?), Willie Phillips.

234. Lancing Minstrels, 1930.

235. Lancing Works Fire Brigade, 1914. Standing (*left to right*): Percy Botting, A. Taylor, Jack Warr, E. Green, Will Morley, H. Harland, G. Young, M. Cluer, Bert Cluer; seated: Charlie Richardson, Dick Dunn, A. Morris, A. H. Panter (Superintendent), Charlie Meads, Bob Dunn, A. Mansfield.

236. Village Fire Brigade, 1920. (*left to right*): Nelson Thorn (Caretaker at the Parish Hall), George 'Slug' Saddler, Ted Comper, Harry Potter (on the ladder), Charlie Potter, Ted Battrick, Councillor John Neil, Chief Officer Charlie Page.

237. Village Fire Brigade outside the old Fire Station in North Road, 1928. (*left to right*): Bob Dunn (plumber), Fred Peters (baker), Bill Cook (chauffeur to the Neil family), Alf Aitken (baker for Pages), Reg Page (baker and Captain of Works Fire Brigade at this time), Horace Trott (farm worker for Phillips), Stan Phillips (farmer), Jack Trevett.

LANCING HOSPITAL PARADES

Before the days of the National Health Service, much of the money needed to run hospitals had to be raised by voluntary activities, and a Carnival Parade was held in Lancing each year for this purpose. Such parades persist today in the form of University Rag Weeks and other similar activities.

238. Carnival Parade July 1924.

239. Hospital Parade, 1912.

240. Parade on 2 June 1912 passing the site which was to be occupied by the parish hall and St. Michaels church.

241. Parade in the 1920s at the same place as above, but with the new buildings erected.

242. Men's stag outing from the *Farmers*, 1910.

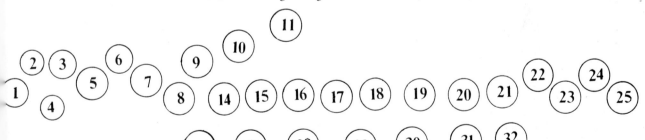

1. Mr. Feldwick (Builder and Undertaker)
2. Charlie Pycroft (Market Gardener)
3. David Snelling (Butcher)
4. Ted Feldwick (son of No. 1)
5. ?
6. ?
7. ?
8. Leo Prideaux (Landlord of *The Horseshoes*)
9. George Marchant (Building Trade)
10. Alick Page (Baker)
11. Percy Lynn (Landlord of *The Farmers*)
12. Mrs. Lynn (At window on balcony)
13. Young lady at window
14. George Gammans
15. Walter Colbourne (Draper)
16. Guy Gibbs
17. Arthur Hollindale (Carter for Fullers)
18. Bert Lisher
19. Tom Till
20. Will Trevett (Cabman)
21. Edwin Fuller (Market Gardener)
22. Joe Bolt (Market Gardener)
23. Martin Fuller (Market Gardener)
24. ?
25. Will Gammans (Coalman)
26. Fred Fuller
27. Bill Chandler (Estate Agent)
28. Tom Hardy
29. Tommy Luckin (Butcher)
30. Martin Fuller senior (Market Gardener)
31. Mr. Nicholson
32. Albert Young (Insurance Agent)

XVI SOUTHERN RAILWAY WORKS

The Railway carriage works, which were concerned with the making and repair of rolling stock, were transferred from Brighton to Lancing in 1910, and their gradually-increasing size and importance had a major effect on the population of the village. New housing estates were developed to accommodate the influx of workers, and the various nurseries were sold off as building sites. After the nationalisation of the railways, a redistribution of activities took place, and in 1965 the carriage works were transferred to Eastleigh in Hampshire, and the site was developed as the Churchill Industrial Estate, for light engineering and other commerical enterprises.

243. (*above*) Carriage works from the air.

244. (*right*) Interior of the carriage works.

245. (*below*) External view of carriage works.

246. (*above left*) The water tower, which gave its name to Tower Road, was built to supply water to the carriage works. Water was pumped from a borehole some 300 ft. below the tower, and stored in the tank.

247. (*above right*) The tank became redundant with the closure of the works and was knocked down in 1968.

248. The waggon shop staff in 1912. Notice the standardised appearance, cloth cap and moustache!

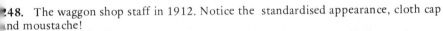

249. The Works Brass Band was a flourishing activity under its Bandmaster, Mr. Bond, winning a number of competitions over the years.

250. (*above*) One branch of the Lisher family were coal merchants. Here we see Mary Lisher outside the coal office, now Corralls, in the late 1920s. The price of coal was 46s and 49s per ton.

251. (*right*) Lisher's coal cart with Hubert Lisher and Bill Guy.

There were five large farms in the Lancing area, the College Farm, Church Farm, Monks Farm, Culverhouse Farm and Old and New Salts Farm, together with three smaller ones, Bushby's Homestead in South Street, Lishers in Freshbrook and Marshalls in North Lancing.

The main produce from the market gardens were grapes, peaches, tomatoes, cucumbers, figs, melons and various vegetables. The flower crop consisted of lilies, geraniums, chrysanthemums and daffodils. These crops were sent by rail to Covent Garden and some by horse-drawn vans to Brighton market.

During the winter, loads of seaweed were taken from the beach and used as manure for the crops.

252. The staff of Gooderams nurseries, 1910. (*left to right*) standing: Fred Sievier, Joe Thorn, George Foster, (?); seated: Ted Merriott, Alfred Strudwick, (?).

253. Picking flowers at Phillips.

254. Packing flowers for market at Gooderams.

255. Fullers Vineries, Penhill Road This is now the Ingleside estate.

256. Fruit picking at Fullers nurseries, 1912. (*left to right*)· Mr. Nidder, Martin Fuller jnr. (*above*), Tom Boyd (*below*), Hector Boyd, Frank Fuller, Edwin Fuller, Martin Fuller snr.

BRICKMAKING

Brickmaking took place in Lancing between 1888 and 1913, when the claypits were exhausted and the industry had to close down.

The brickworks with its kilns or stacks were in Penhill Road and at its peak the output was between 28,000 and 32,000 bricks per week. The men worked ten-hour shifts, and of this about one and a half hours would be spent in the actual process of making bricks, and the rest of the time on the preparation and clearing up. The finished bricks were dispatched by rail, and the goods yard at Lancing station was a very busy place in those days. Some were dispatched locally by horse and cart.

INDEX OF PERSONS

Arabic numbers denote a plate number, Roman numerals an Introduction